VOICE OVER SECRETS

22 SUCCESSFUL VOICE ACTORS & VOICE OVER ARTISTS SHARE THEIR BEST EXPERIENCE-BASED TIPS

info@thesuccesstips.com thesuccesstips.com
ISBN 978-1-8383708-0-0 (Paper Back)
ISBN 978-1-8383708-1-7 (Kindle)
ISBN 978-1-8383708-2-4 (Audible)
Published by FAADA
Editor: Elroy 'Spoonface' Powell

Contributors: Abi Phillips, Alex Maude, Bhav Parmar, Carrie Afrin, Clare Reeves, Daisy Porter, Daniel Relf, Della Phillips, Donna-Louise Bryan, Elisabeth Valentine, Emma Wheeler, Lorraine Ansell, Lucy Ellis, Malk Williams, Mel Parker, Nano Nagle, Noelle Adames, Paul Rose, Ramesh Mahtani, Thomas Machin and Vicky Tessio.

A CIP catalogue record for this book is available from the British Library.

DISCLAIMER

Secrets of a Voice-Over Professional is intended for information purposes only. This book does not constitute specific advice unique to your situation. The views and opinions expressed in this book are those of the contributing authors and do not reflect those of the Publisher. The Editor, Contributing Authors, Publisher and Resellers accept no responsibility for loss, damage or injury to persons or their belongings as a direct or indirect result of reading this book.

All people mentioned in the case studies have been used with permission and have had their names, genders, industries and personal details altered to protect client confidentiality and privacy. Any resemblance to persons living or dead is purely coincidental.

We have made every attempt to locate the copyright holders of the additional material available on copyright free sites and we will amend any future revisions of this book if new information arises.

WELCOME TO VOICE OVER SECRETS: 22 SUCCESSFUL VOICE ACTORS & VOICE OVER ARTISTS SHARE THEIR BEST EXPERIENCE-BASED TIPS

Hi. I'm Elroy 'Spoonface' Powell, Spoon The Voice Guy, and thank you for picking up this earthy guide aimed at giving new voice-over artists and voice actors field tested and experience-based insights.

Creating your own definition of success in the industry is important. From the 'secrets' shared here, it certainly is about more than having a 'great voice'.

This book brings together a diverse collection of some of the best professional voices.

I asked them all the same three questions and the answers that came back were so colourful, varied and inspirational. They have been kind enough to share their own personal adventures. Honest and easy to digest, please allow yourself to explore these gems with an open mind and the willingness to borrow the best bits for your own journey.

The voice-over industry comes with a high barrier to entry and it can seem very hard to access. What training is required? How much equipment is enough? Do you need an agent?

One thing for sure is that there is no one size fits all approach, although there are a few considerations in order to form a strong foundation for the best chance of a sustainable career.

Join our mailing list for more information and drop me a line via social media if you have any questions.

https://thesuccesstips.com / @spoonface1

5 TIPS FOR NEW VOICE-OVER ARTISTS

According to a 2017Voices report, the industry is worth $4.4 billion globally.

With multiple global 'lockdowns' in 2020 came the harsh reality for some that they could no longer trade the way they had before. The Office for National Statistics (ONS) stated that 156,000 people were made redundant from April to July (UK).

Already working from home, many voice artists found that the demand for voice acting / voice-over services, on the contrary, exploded exponentially. This was especially true for experienced and well-established voice actors with professional home studios.

With that in mind, here are 5 tips that we hope you will find useful:

1. Make sure that you have the right equipment and know-how to record and deliver to a professional standard. Your clients will not be happy with sub-standard performances and files.
2. Develop and maintain your skills. Stay up to date with the latest trends and keep learning.
3. Update / build your website and social accounts in order to clearly show how you can create a solution for your potential clients. Make it easy to find your services and give your clients what they want.
4. Reach out to your ideal clients but start in your own network and ripple out.
5. Actively engage in the practice of mindfulness to help you through the challenges and to avoid burnout. This is the most important. Be prepared for the long game while reviewing your quality of life with an awareness of where you are at with your inner peace. Does it feel right for you?

6 CONSIDERATIONS FOR VOICE ACTORS THAT HAVE AN AGENT

An agent is often highly revered and seen as a proverbial knight in shining armour able to make it rain bookings. The truth is, only a small amount of artists on any roster get the majority of the work. But why? You have a great voice and your agent is so connected. So what is the problem?

1. Clients want who they want.

Your voice just may not be suitable for that particular brand, product or service. Also, to save time and money, it often makes sense to go back to an artist that they've worked with previously.

2. Are there too many voices?

On a large roster, the attention is divided among all of the other voices hungry for work.

3. Are your career goals aligned with your agent's business model?

You may have grand ideas about where you see yourself (and rightly so) but if your agent is not on the same page, both of you will hit a wall of frustration.

4. Are you in a non-exclusive deal?

Flexibility is great but the lack of commitment can also result in your agent not having to work hard enough for you. It takes time to service your reels and promote you. Patience and managing expectations, especially in the early days, is so important.

Nonetheless, a flexible exclusive deal means that win-win opportunities can be negotiated but still require an agent to push your career or risk losing you.

5. Are you proactive enough?

You need to take responsibility for building your authority and influence. If you're not running your own paid ads, making videos, podcasts, collaborating and creating a presence in other areas, you'll be left behind and the best agent in the world will struggle to get you work.

6. Are you actively engaging in a practice of mindfulness to deal with the challenges and avoid burnout?

None of the above matters if we're unable to overcome our fear of potential ridicule, perceived failure, running out of money, self-doubt and anything else that gets in the way of forging a sustainable career.

Allow that to swirl for a moment and let's head over to our collection of shared wisdom so you can make up your own mind.

In alphabetical order, many thanks go to Abi Phillips, Alex Maude, Bhav Parmar, Carrie Afrin, Clare Reeves, Daisy Porter, Daniel Relf, Della Phillips, Donna-Louise Bryan, Elisabeth Valentine, Emma Wheeler, Lorraine Ansell, Lucy Ellis, Malk Williams, Mel Parker, Nano Nagle, Noelle Adames, Paul Rose, Ramesh Mahtani, Thomas Machin and Vicky Tessio.

CONTENTS

ABI PHILLIPS

I've been voicing professionally for over 11 years now, so I have faced many challenges as one does, no matter the industry or career path that they have chosen. My biggest challenge to date is actually one that I'm facing currently. I was recently cast as the voice for a TV Campaign for a very well-known client. Unfortunately, this particular commercial has spiked public controversy due to the nature and tone of the ad regarding its subject. As sometimes happens in our industry, the script wasn't released to me until I was in the studio with the end-client and sound engineer. Upon initially reading it, I hadn't realised quite how controversial it was. My job is to deliver what my client is asking for and to give my absolute best performance no matter my opinion of the content. This is what I did. However, to see your work being publicly pulled apart is really something that I had never considered that I may be faced with and nothing can prepare you for it. I wasn't expecting the reaction that it prompted. It really upset me. The most important thing to remember when you are a performer, whether that is in front of the camera, on stage or behind a microphone, is that there may come a time when you or something you have been involved with comes under scrutiny. It is the way you handle this that determines whether you are directly affected by it or not. It was easy to get upset; I had worked hard on this campaign, as I always do, so to see it being ridiculed really hurt my feelings. But that is exactly the point.

Our work as voice-over artists is not about US. It's not about our personal feelings or opinions. It's about delivering the job we are hired to do to the best of our ability. All I can do in this situation is learn from it. It isn't always in your control to pick and choose the projects you are involved with. Sometimes you have to negotiate and/or agree to the job before you are shown the content of the script, that's just the way it goes. The most important thing to remember is that your work is NOT you. You cannot afford to take things personally. At the end of the day, I did my job, I did it well, the content of the commercial was not my decision to make and the criticism it received was not down to my performance. I have had to toughen myself up, grow a thick skin and remind myself that when you choose a career in the public domain, there will be times when things happen that are outside of your control or that won't please everyone. You just have to roll with it!

I have been very lucky in my time as a voice-over artist to work with some incredibly kind people as well as reputable and well-respected companies and brands. I have also been given the opportunity to challenge myself creatively and that is any performers' dream. As a primarily commercial/promotional artist, I am used to receiving upbeat, salesy scripts where the aim is to make the product sound like the most exciting and incredible thing I've ever come across. This is great fun and I love to do it but my favourite project by far was very different. I voiced a Web Commercial with a European client for Schwarzkopf Professional about a year and a half ago, and I was instantly buzzing to get started on it. They wanted a sultry read, something soft and enticing. This is a voicing style I have always wanted to get my teeth into! It was hard. It pushed me outside of my comfort zone but it showed me what I was capable of. It ended up being nominated for a 2020 One Voice Award for Best Web Commercial! Being nominated for, or winning, awards is not what my work is about but it definitely reassures me that when I think I've done a good job, someone else may think so too and I may even be commended for it!

When I first started voicing, I was 14 years old. I was convinced by the age of 8 that I would one day be an actress in the West End (despite the fact that I can't sing or dance but hey, maybe that's why it never happened)! I had big dreams as many young people do. I wanted to be the best actress that ever lived – I soon realised this may not be my reality but if I could go back and talk to myself then, I would tell myself not to be disheartened by this. I was lucky to have found my calling and to know what I wanted to do at such a young age. I would also tell myself to rise above the scepticism I would inevitably receive. The number of times I was asked while studying acting at school and college, while doing performing arts at University and ultimately when I evolved my part-time voice-over career to a full-time one in 2016, "Do you really think you'll ever be successful though?" or "Will you really make any money from that?" I couldn't tell you. There were times when it really hurt me. It saddened me that because I wasn't following the usual or expected path, people couldn't seem to take me seriously. But I would tell myself to use that feeling to my advantage as I continue to do now! No matter what you do in life, there will always be someone there to tell you you're doing it wrong or that it's not what they would do – but that's why they're not the one doing it. I was meant to do this and I love doing it. I consider myself one of the luckiest people in the world to be able to say I've never hated a day at work.

BIO:

Abi is a youthful, vibrant, professional British voice-over artist with a broadcast-quality home studio based in Essex, just outside of London. Her husky, cool and friendly tone lends itself well to Radio and TV Commercials, Imaging, Sponsorship and Promotions, IVR, e-Learning and Corporate Narration. Her background in acting makes her a great choice for Character Performances, whether they be wacky cartoon voices or relatable real-life characters. Her clients describe her as a 'versatile fresh-breath' who delivers outstanding audio every time.

Links:

- https://twitter.com/voiceoverabi
- https://www.instagram.com/voiceoverabi/
- https://www.linkedin.com/in/abi-phillips-voice-over/?originalSubdomain=uk

ALEX MAUDE

In an industry where self-motivation is king, perfectionism and imposter syndrome are the lying advisors that whisper in your ear.

And they're damn convincing too, with old favourites like dismissing your own achievements, demanding to know why you're not booked up for the next five years with gigs and if you never try you can never fail, among others.

These are things I find constantly popping up. Why do these people want to work with me? Why is my opinion being considered on a similar level to these experts? I am always questioning and doubting instead of accepting.

It's an odd cognitive dissonance as I have a firm belief in my own acting ability (more to follow on that) but often feel like a child when navigating the practical aspects of the industry. Put me in front of a mic and I'll portray any kind of character you throw at me but ask me how to get in front of said mic and I'm like... what's an e-mail? Obviously that's comic hyperbole but it's what I feel like sometimes.

So how have I overcome this major stumbling block that is standing in the way of proverbial (or literal) world domination? The truth is... I haven't yet.

That, I feel, is a supremely important phrase. Both admitting that I haven't overcome my internal strife (and that that is ok) but also that I haven't done so... *yet.* Hope is a supremely powerful force. True despair lies in hopelessness. If you have hope then you can never truly fall into real darkness. So I am proud of the fact that I have genuine hope that I can improve not only my 'industry navigation' ability but all of my abilities as well!

A new mantra that I have developed of late with my wonderful therapist is change the behaviour and the rest will follow. It can be hard to 'do the thing' (starting things specifically, dear God that is a hard thing for me) but much like stepping out on to stage in front of an audience, once you have started, you *have* to finish. I have found that the anticipation of a thing is often far worse than the thing itself, particularly when it comes to something that one is skilled in. The acting, singing and narrating instincts kick in and the nagging inner critic can't get a word in edgeways.

Don't give in to the inner critic and the lying anxiety. Start the task. Send the email. Give the speech. Record the scene. Write the chapter. Do the thing.

In other words: Change the behaviour and the rest will follow.

I was in this exact same situation not too long ago. I was working with some very high-profile people that I had admired for a long long time. Due to my NDA, names have been seamlessly replaced.

As an avid gamer myself, I have long wanted to lend my voice to video games as I believe there is such great story-telling potential unlike in any other medium. My very first game job was with Games Inc. I had an opportunity to work with a representative of Games Inc, Jane, someone who I have also long admired.

Working with Games Inc has been a *career goal*. I cannot emphasise how excited I was when I got the call. That they had asked for me specifically (having met and worked with Jane previously) was beyond mind-blowing.

The day came and I paced the area around the studio, having turned up a good half an hour early. I was warming up and thinking: How is *this* my first gaming job? This is insane… Oh God I hope I'm good enough that they'll ask me back!

I walk in, passing another actor on their way out who I know. *Oh God… they were working with them… they're so much more prominent than me!* I explained how excited and nervous I was to be working with Jane. They said don't worry, she's lovely (completely true).

However, as I was saying earlier, once I stepped into the booth and started, my aforementioned acting confidence came flooding back! I was able to stand up in front of the world and my legs did not fall out from under me.

I was proud. Still disbelieving and fanboy-ing incredibly hard… but if I can tick off a career goal this early… I can do anything!

Naturally though, my new goal is to work with Games Inc… *again*!

Henry Ford once said: "Nothing is particularly hard if you divide it into small jobs." If I were to advise my past self, I would say don't fear the grandeur of the great and the large. The whole may be greater than the sum of its parts… but it is still the sum of its parts. Rome wasn't built in a day and neither will your career.

Nobody you admire got to where they are today on their first try. Serena Williams didn't develop a supersonic serve on her first swing of a racket.

If you fear the great things that you can envision such as writing a twelve-book epic, voicing a main character for 10 seasons, voicing an iconic character with years of history behind them and so on then you will never achieve them. But if you can view those same grand ideas as so many cogs in a machine, as so many individual words on a page, as so many single steps on a journey of a thousand miles… then it will be much more achievable.

No one said that it wouldn't be devilishly hard but I want to be the king who turns around and says: "There. I walked two miles today!"

"But your Majesty," whisper the lying advisors, "You still have 996 miles to go. That's such a long way! Surely it is better we return to the castle and sit on the throne where it is safe?"

"I may have 996 miles to go," says the king, "but I am four miles further along this journey than when I started. Is that not an achievement to be proud of? Is this not an endeavour that will all be worth it in the end?"

Yes, your Majesty. Yes it will.

BIO:

Alex Maude is a London-based actor and writer. He considers his voice to be one of his strongest assets as an actor along with a vivid imagination and a desire to explore and give the best possible stories to the world. When he isn't acting, Alex likes to keep his voice and brain active by working as a professional Dungeon Master for the popular roleplaying game Dungeons and Dragons.

Links:

- alexmaude.com
- Twitter: @AlexIMaude
- Facebook: @AlexIMaude

BHAV PARMAR

I definitely think that the most challenging experience has been juggling the different hats of being a VO entrepreneur. This includes being the centre of your business and having to manage everything from the performance, business and marketing elements and the technical side of things too (now more than ever!). It all requires time, patience and a lot of conscious training.

These have been positive challenges however. These are ones that allow you to gain all rounded value in relation to your clients and there are the ones that will make you a confident creative once you develop the skills.

Overcoming it involves a few stages. Firstly, understand that these three elements (and the other micro elements associated with this) are part of your everyday work. It is your duty to check that all of them are up to scratch. Be that adapting to new methods of marketing, learning the skills to move into a different area of VO or even mastering your studio and the quality of your audio. Then comes identifying your weak spots. It may be that you are in full flow of having vocal training every week but you are not reaching out to as many new clients as you could be. Having that constant awareness of what is working or not and then refashioning your approach appropriately is really the key. Lastly, you should approach the development of each section with as little risk of overwhelming yourself as possible. Tiny goals and big steps as I like to call it. You should really prioritising which areas need work and set weekly, monthly and yearly tasks for each. One action a day that results in positive progress is an approach that works for developing any part of your work.

What's your favourite project?

Oh there have been many! I have loved working on a couple of PS4 titles this year and a new animation on Amazon Prime called Uma and Devan: Namate – a great educational show!

The most fun I have had was on a new VR educational project that I embarked on with a fab production company and an old time friend! Although I cannot disclose the name, it is a revolutionary approach to interactive learning and uses VR for essentially saving lives.

The reason why I loved it so much and am still loving it (we are running through 2021!) is because it allows me to play a character that I probably would not have been cast for on camera. A witty agent and sidekick! It brings together comedy and drama in a way that gives access to vital learning.

Working with new technology is so exciting. It really keeps me on the cusp of understanding trends in the VO world and how are our voices are so powerful and inherent to education. Above that, my good friend is directing the whole project which brings with it a sense of chemistry and flavour to the character that I would have otherwise not been able to explore. We have both embarked on a collaborative process and the input that I am able to give and how we are able to play off one another makes the character so distinct and enjoyable to perform!

This project has taught me a lot about myself too such as pushing my boundaries in performance, how to work remotely and how the process of VR production takes place. Understanding how you fit into the bigger picture of a project is really empowering and it allows you to apply yourself with a lot more confidence. I know that the future of this project means more fun and more chances for me to develop my all round skills in VO - that's enough to make any project a favourite!

What would I tell myself if I could go back to when I first started?

Relax girl, it's all going to be OK. Not everything will make sense at every stage but work hard, be you and move forward.

When you read through lots of interviews from bigger celebs, you hear this time and time again and for good and real reason. It's so important to be ok with where you are at, I think. Don't continually compare yourself to others. You are on your own journey and that is ok. The more you accept this, the better your energy is placed.

It's scary sometimes not knowing what the future holds as a creative but embrace that. If you are doing the work you love with the people you love, then you are in the right place.

I would also tell myself to be more fearless and to be willing to take risks in auditions. It may seem counterintuitive when you are building your work and finances. You don't want to put yourself out but those dive-ins really equate to growth and it is that growth that is very liberating and strengthening when it comes to choosing the work that you want to be known for.

Finally, place yourself at the heart of every piece of work that you do. Write down 5 things about yourself that you are proud of. Your words should describe you. Actively place those idiosyncrasies, quirks and characters into your work. That's what people are looking for. The earlier you can be comfortable with sharing that, the more free and confident you will be in your art.

BIO:

Bhavnisha is an actress and voice-over artist best known for her work in the latest seasons of Doctor Who playing the fun and witty Sonya Khan. This is as well as the award winning web series Brothers With No Game, Darren Has a Breakdown and film drama Aami and Frank playing opposite Ricci Harnett. Other screen credits include the BBC, Sony, Samsung, War Child and To Die For (Cannes).

Behind the mic, Bhavnisha has a warm, reassuring and conversational tone with a youthful intelligence and witty charm. She has worked with companies globally and locally such as Apple, Twitter, Expedia, Panasonic, Braun, the BBC, Audible India, Goldman Sachs, Royal Mail and HSBC. These include Commercials, Animations, Films, Audiobooks, VR Technologies and Documentaries. Bhavnisha is currently playing the mum in the Amazon Prime animation Uma and Devan. She is both the voice of Apple India and a new VR Learning system to be released next year.

Links:

- www.voiceofbhavnisha.com
- www.bhavnishaparmar.com
- Instagram: @bhavnishaparmar: https://www.instagram.com/bhavnisha_parmar/?hl=en
- LinkedIn: Bhavnisha Parmar: https://www.linkedin.com/in/bhavnishaparmar/
- Twitter: @BhavnishaP - https://twitter.com/BhavnishaP

QUESTION:

What got you interested in the voice over industry?

Drop a tweet @spoonface1 and let's discuss…

CARRIE AFRIN

Prior to joining the voice-over world, I worked in Finance. I had always been part of a team, sometimes large and sometimes small but either way, I had a supervisor to help me make decisions and colleagues to discuss my work with. My most challenging experience in the voice industry was that suddenly it was only me in my team. I had to make all of the decisions by myself. You find yourself becoming the designer of your recording space and the quality controller on the audio that you produce. You make the decisions on what your website should include and all marketing posts. All of a sudden, you are in charge of the financial side of your business such as having to ensure that you comply with the accounting requirements and managing your budget appropriately. Like many self-employed people, you will find that you have to wear a lot of different hats and all of them well. Some of these skills were brand new to me so there was a lot to learn all at once with no supervisors or colleagues to brainstorm with or run my ideas past. I really struggled with that.

When working in the bank, I used to get monthly reviews from my supervisor and one recurring point that kept coming up was that I should have more confidence in my decision-making. Instead of coming up with a plan and just doing it, I'd always check it by a colleague or team leader first instead of just trusting my own judgement.

When I first started in the voice-over industry, this was a real sticking point. I would interpret the script and record the piece but during the editing process, I'd start to doubt either the delivery style or my interpretation of the script. On some occasions, I'd even start all over again, only to find myself going back to the first version and being pleased with that.

I knew that my confidence in decision-making was really holding me back so I started to look online for ways to fix the issue. One thing that really helped was leaving space between recording and editing. Where time allowed, I would record the script and then leave it for an hour before going back to edit. This really helped and I kept telling myself (sometimes out loud) to trust my own judgement and try not to overthink things.

Then I had a real breakthrough… I was contacted by another VO who invited me to a Google Hangout with a group of VO's that they met regularly with. It was brilliant to speak with others in the industry and to bounce ideas off one another. For years now, we have been meeting online for a regular monthly call and I have found them to be a fantastic support network. Sometimes we just meet for a blether about work that month and other times we choose specific topics to discuss such as editing techniques or marketing.

We all started our VO careers at a similar time and as we all have different skills and strengths, this collaboration has been a great asset over the years. Debby and Mike are American, Mel, Steve and Guy are English and I am the token Scot of the group. I would highly recommend to anyone starting out in VO that you find a small group of people at a similar stage to yourself and team up. Having a support network has been invaluable to me over the years.

One of my favourite things about working in the voice-over industry is that I am constantly learning new things. Each script tells me something new - this can range from the price of cheese in the supermarket to a complicated medical procedure. My favourite projects are e-learning courses as I get to learn the most from these scripts. I particularly love the business and personal growth topics. Other topics such as North Sea Drilling techniques might not have quite the same buzz or retention but it is still fascinating to read about. One medical script that I found particularly intriguing explored the links between childhood trauma and chronic illness in adults. I had never even heard of the topic before reading that script. I feel very lucky to be in a job where I can learn as I work.

What would I tell myself to do differently if I could go back to the start?

I would say "invest in training from the very beginning." When I first started out, I spent a lot of time on teaching myself different VO techniques via books and internet research. However, this is not nearly as effective as investing in professional training. By working with a coach or completing a VO course, this will allow you to get that all-important feedback from an instructor with the opportunity for a two-way dialog. This really is invaluable! I found that the feedback was such a boost to my confidence and if there were skills I needed to work on then I could go away and focus my homework on these key areas. I do regret not getting training from day 1. It would have made the initial start-up process a lot easier.

BIO:

Carrie Afrin is a Scottish voice-over artist based in the Highlands. With a friendly, caring and trustworthy voice, Carrie can help you to describe, inform and sell or simply answer your phone with her friendly voice.

Her CV includes Boots, HSBC, Scotmid, Tulloch Homes, Cancer Research and many more. Carrie is also a fluent Gaelic Speaker.

Links:

- carriesvoice.co.uk
- https://twitter.com/carries_voice
- https://www.instagram.com/carriesvoice/

CLARE REEVES

When I moved into being a full time voice-over artist about 11 years ago, it took me a good while (possibly 2 years or so) to feel confident that I actually WAS a voice-over artist! My career up to this point had been in radio as a presenter and sound engineer, in addition to working in TV directing channels for the BBC. I had in fact been voicing things for years way before I became a VO but for some reason, I didn't feel legit. This was my most challenging experience in the VO industry. I felt that I needed to keep a fairly low profile while I learned more, built a client base up and felt at ease in my sound. I wanted to be "good enough" before daring to attend any VO events. As little as 10 years ago, the industry felt like a very different place. It was more closed and the opportunities for training and learning were fewer and harder to find. It felt like trying to solve a puzzle. On my own, I solved it by speaking to a couple of VOs that I had known for a while. I also worked VERY HARD behind the scenes to find work using my existing media contacts, identified my strengths and weaknesses and carved out a place for myself in the industry to a point of feeling credible enough to own the title 'Voice-Over Artist'. I feel very strongly that anyone coming into the business should respect the work that goes into being successful as a VO. If they are going to own the title, they need to match the professionalism of their peers.

I have been fortunate enough to have worked on a range of exciting and fun projects as a voice-over artist from TV commercials to documentary narration, ADR and more. If I had to choose one favourite, it would probably be the night that I was the live Voice of God (announcer) at the AIM Independent Music Awards. This was a very cool music industry event and being part of that felt so exciting. I live announced the on stage hosts, (Radio 1 DJs I ate lasagne with backstage before the show!) guests, the nominated acts and winners as well as the performers for the night. Over that evening, I announced the likes of Jarvis Cocker, Stormzy, Public Service Broadcasting and Nick Cave! As someone with a background in live broadcasting and a love of music, this felt like the perfect project for me. I was able to draw on my strengths and years of experience to do a good job and pull the event together with my voice. Hugely satisfying and great fun.

What if I knew then what you know now?

The route I took actually worked for me. I would still quietly build up my work, confidence and skills behind the scenes. I think that I would possibly start thinking sooner about what my voice worked well for project-wise and where my strengths and skillsets were in order to fully embrace them sooner. I don't think I expected to work as much as I do within the corporate sector but it turns out that my sound and delivery work well for large tech and pharmaceutical companies!

I might have started attending voice-over events sooner as well. I made some great friends that way.

BIO:

Clare was born in Torquay, Devon. After training in theatre and media, Clare worked for the BBC for a number of years as a Radio Presenter, sound engineer, TV Channel Director and running internal BBC training.

Clare founded her voice-over business in 2010. Her background in broadcasting - from both sides of the microphone - gives her a real edge in the voice-over world where she brings her unique knowledge of the world of broadcasting into everything she does.

Living on the Kent coast, Clare is a keen sea swimmer and a player of alto and baritone saxophones, bringing fresh air and musicality into her work and making waves with words.

Clare's voice-over clients include Colgate, Bosch, Facebook, Hyundai, Booking.com, National Geographic and Clearblue.

Links:

- www.clarereevesvoiceovers.com
- Twitter @clareonairlive
- Instagram @clarereevesvoiceovers

DAISY PORTER

In my head, a voice-over career involved breezing into a studio in a trendy part of London with an annotated script in one hand and a lemon tea in the other, completing the job (in half the booked time, of course) and leaving with a handshake and a smile, already thinking of that juicy invoice to be written in Pret half an hour later.

Of course, all of that would change when I finally saved up for a home studio and started recording from home, made unlistenable recordings, getting tangled up in wires, failing horribly and realising just how clueless and inexperienced I really was.

In the studio, the sound engineer and client are on the other end to take care of all of the tech and to offer direction - mostly helpful of course, although I do enjoy the occasional baffling comment of 'Can you do it slower but with more speed?' In a home studio though, it's just you and the microphone. When combined with a tight deadline, a sluggish internet and a faint buzzing noise that you just can't figure out to remove, it can be a complete disaster.

The shift from being the voice artist who breezes in, does the job and leaves the rest to the professionals to my sudden promotion to Director, Sound Engineer and Technician was utterly terrifying. I realised very quickly how little I actually knew. As a result, it would take me hours to get a job done as I'd overcompensate, overanalyse and underserve.

The way I got over it, frankly, was by sucking up, leaving my ego at the door and getting on with it. When you're self-directing, it's so easy to veer into over-analytical mode as there's a fine line between constructive self-criticism and overindulgent self-flagellation. Was that S a little too sharp? That phrase a little over-egged? It's not long before ear fatigue sets in and the ability to discern between takes becomes slippier than a Salvador Dali painting.

Pace yourself. Do three takes. Listen to them. Then do three more. Listen to them. Set yourself a time limit so then you're not going to tear your hair out over that tiny difference between Take 6 and Take 12. Trust in your own abilities.

What I ended up realising to do with the joy of the home studio is having the autonomy and opportunity to work and perfect your skills. The only time I could properly work on my voice was when I'd already booked the job and was in the studio (which, listening back now, really didn't lead to my best work). Now, each new audition or demo that comes in is like a trip to the gym. It is a new challenge and an opportunity to grow and get a little bit better at noticing that slightly sibilant S, that over-pronounced P and that gorgeous little inflection on the end of the last sentence that just might clinch you the job. I've learnt more in the year that I've been recording from home than in the last three years put together.

Do I love the studio?

Yes. But do I love *my* studio? Absolutely.

Most of my work comes from the commercial and corporate sector - which I absolutely adore - but I really relish the opportunity to play around as much as possible and to explore the versatility of my voice.

When Spoon asked me to come on board for *Love Jumps* Season 1, I had no idea what to expect, especially as the dialogue and scenarios would be mostly improvised. I voiced multiple characters in *Love Jumps* - including Dani, who is similar to my own voice - but I also played some of the supporting characters which ranged from a faint caricature to the truly bizarre. There's one recurring bit in the show where some anthropomorphic objects of a Dani's handbag converse with each other. We were allowed to pick which everyday objects we'd like to voice. So, naturally, I chose to play the spare tampon hidden for emergencies in the inside pocket.

Then comes the fun bit – what voice to do? I thought about what a ratty, own-brand tampon would be like – female and somewhat decrepit but with a wicked sense of humour. Suddenly this hoarse, weary New York accent that had been smoking Silk Cut from birth started leaving my mouth. Aha! She's alive! And with a laugh that sounds like Krusty the Clown choking on a Scotch Bonnet!

Doing *Love Jumps* is a clear reminder that the best part of character acting is that nobody can be sure what the actor looks like. That's where the fun really is – especially when you're pretending to be a lewd old sanitary product.

What would I do differently?

The short answer? Buy a home studio earlier. Be more proactive. Don't be afraid to ask for advice. Don't be afraid, full stop.

But to be really honest - and I'll whisper into the mike for this one – I wouldn't tell myself to do anything differently. Even the failures and the fuck-ups. Those failures have been the strongest and most important learning experiences of my career.

When I finished drama school, I posted in a popular Facebook group for voice-over artists to ask for some advice about demo reels. The responses I got were, 'If you have to ask for advice, you're probably not ready or experienced enough' – which were, looking back, disappointing and frankly unhelpful. I know what those comments were trying to say but if you wait until you think you're ready or experienced enough, you probably never will be.

Really, isn't that why we choose to be voice artists? To put ourselves out there boldly, not knowing what might happen, knowing that things might not work out the way we want them too but also knowing that's the beauty of it all?

BIO:

Daisy is a voice-over artist who specialises in commercials and corporate readings. Her voice has been described as warm, reassuring and velvety. Her previous clients include Churchill, Epson, Agrovision and M&S – yes, that voice…

Daisy Porter is also an actress known for Nightmuse (2019), Mediated (2014) and A Call to Arms (2018).

Reviews of her previous work:
'The lightening-sharp marvel that is Daisy Porter' (Everything Theatre)
'Daisy Porter positively lit up the stage with her poise and presence' (Carns Theatre Passion)
'Scenes involving Porter provide a masterclass in acting' (Remote Goat)

- Spotlight: www.spotlight.com/6572-4535-2749
- Twitter: @DaisyPorts
- Agent: spoonsvoices.com

DANIEL RELF

My most challenging experience was making the leap from being a studio engineer to doing voice-over work as a job. This was mostly because I was coming from one side of the microphone, where cost was always a larger factor over creativity, but also because at the time I was still trying to figure out and truly understand my self-worth, both as a voice-over and as a 20 year old guy.

My first job out of university, after studying music technology, was working as a studio engineer for a large on hold based company. The job included duties such as editing, recording and creating on hold promos for a wide range of businesses. Firstly, I was the middle man to record voice-overs at a company approved rate but also to make the voice-overs happy with the rate they received as well. As the turnaround time started to be pushed to two hours, which we couldn't pay too much, the company decided to have in-house talent to record emergency short notice work and then to record with the actual voice-over in the usual time frame. This consisted of anyone with a good phone manner being used, which was three people including myself. We were also offered a little extra money. However, they turned to me and because I was the only one working in the studio, they confirmed that they felt it was part of my existing duties and I was to not get paid for it. Also, if I refused, it would be deemed to not comply with my contract.

This was pretty damaging to my own self-worth, both on a professional level but also on a personal level at such a young age when I was still growing as a person and trying to grasp what this meant.

Not long after this happened, I eventually stopped working for this company and started doing my own thing. This was after having conversations with other voices that had been in the industry for some time who I considered my friends. I have no bad feelings about any of this. It was just part of my journey as I continued to grow as a person.

But with all of this together, for me at the time, this was the most challenging thing I had encountered so far. Maybe if I went through this now, I wouldn't consider this to be a difficult thing but at the time, it really challenged the way that I needed to look at myself, value myself, re-evaluate what I was doing and what I could and would bring to the table regarding my skills.

I've been so lucky to have been involved in a mixture of projects over the years and each one has been enjoyable, even the day to day ones, as it makes no day the same. I would say that I couldn't label this down to just one project as there are two that stick out to me and make me feel lucky to be involved with this industry. The first one I can't mention by name as I am currently under an NDA but it was my first video game AAA title. It isn't a big character either but my teenage years were spent growing up playing video games, so this was sort of my dream of dreams to be involved with a game. This finally happened for me. The small team working on this had just as much enthusiasm and drive for the project which made it a fun thing to be a part of.

The other one, which I can talk about, was my first proper script (I even have it framed). However, it wasn't the fact that I did my first script - it was who the script was for. It was for one of the main sponsors of the Nickelodeon Kid's Choice Awards 2010. It was very surreal to me being able to voice this. To link this in to the most challenging things I have faced, this helped me to see that actually, I am good enough to work with and get paid for working with higher calibre businesses. They came back with the feedback that they loved the excitement that I brought to the script.

One piece of advice that I wish I had taken on earlier which really took me a long time to understand and break the habit of was to go full time into voicing. Voicing for me has always been one of two jobs. This wasn't because of not believing in myself but because everyone in my family has always drilled into me from an early age that you need a stable job. A stable job is one of the most important things that you can have. But a stable job to my family is working for someone else. If you look at how much things have changed, working for yourself is probably more of a stable job as you control the work flow, the creativeness and the work/life balance a lot more. Plus it seems that so many people are easily expendable nowadays.

BIO:

Daniel Alan Relf, born 9th April 1989. His current resume includes work for Apple, Nickelodeon Kid's Choice Awards, BT, Bupa, a currently unreleased AAA title game, plus acting work in various shorts, and motion capture for League of Legends.

Twitter:
@VoiceOverLad

Instagram:
@wreckitrelf_

DELLA PHILLIPS

When I first started out as a professional VO, I came from a Sales and Marketing corporate background which was extremely helpful for self-promotion. Although I'd been acting for the best part of my young life, I didn't go to acting school. I had oodles of experience in plays and monologues etc and I felt like I was a born actor. I would always do accents and silly voices. From a very early age, I was always extremely confident and loud, the life and soul of the party, goofing around and being a clown, so much so that I got myself into a lot of trouble at school. As my father was my headmaster, it really didn't go down too well!

However, once I left the corporate world behind and started out in this very competitive field, I found that I would be judged and sometimes felt "not worthy" as I hadn't gone to drama school which knocked my confidence. I threw myself into studying acting techniques and practiced on video before watching myself back. I was very self-critical and at times, I don't think it did my confidence much good. I have always been a bit of a perfectionist – I was brought up with the attitude "If a job's worth doing, it's worth doing well", which I'm very grateful for. However, it also made me have a slight insecurity about whether my best was good enough.

I have done a lot of training since then and I really believe that if you can contact someone who is an expert in their craft and learn something from them, it will help you to find your comfort zone. For me, I learned that it's OK not to feel a master at everything. Once I found my niche with help from others, my career started to soar. I also like to surround myself with like-minded positive people who are happy for my success and can share in it, rather than begrudging my success. I have no time for negativity. It's destructive and makes me sad. I love to network with my peers and I think that in the VO industry, we are very lucky to have such a supportive group of people. During lockdown, it's been hard not being able to socialise with them as usual but thank goodness for Zoom, I have done some fabulous online courses and attended some lovely social gatherings. All of this helps to build your self-worth and self-belief.

My favourite project has to be the radio commercial I recorded for the Samaritans with Tom Marshall, a producer from S2Blue. I also won an award for voicing it at the 2018 One Voice Awards for Best Female Radio Commercial. That's not why it's my favourite, although of course I'm chuffed to have won an award. Mental health has always been important to me since I was a child and also since losing our 17 year old daughter in a car accident in 2005. I think that the Samaritans do an incredible job and I have no problem sharing that I phoned them in the past when I had my very dark moments. When I felt that life was challenging, they helped me enormously. To voice an advert for the very people who helped me to value myself at one of the most difficult times in my life was an honour and a privilege. When I listen to it, the hairs stand up on the back of my neck. It's very simple and no effects. Just my voice and a simple piano bed. You can hear the emotion in my voice - it's genuine and moving.

I think that for the first few years, I was obsessed with having to find an agent, otherwise I might not be considered professional. I almost became desperate about it but I think that really, it's just as important to study your craft, to work hard networking and to audition for as many jobs as you can. I think that once you've mastered what you do and know your strengths and weaknesses, the rest will come. As a "newbie" I hadn't really appreciated the equity rates and industry rates. I wish I'd understood and learned those better. Nowadays, there is a lot more support in this area and it's so important to ensure that you are being paid what you're worth. Once I got my head around that, I became a lot more confident in knowing my worth and I would urge people new to the industry to ensure that they don't undersell themselves. This is also important as it ensures that our industry maintains high standard rates for us all. If people work for low rates, it brings down the rates for all of us. I would say, believe in yourself and work hard. Once you are ready, you will be able to get an agent but it's not imperative.

BIO:

Della is a busy professional award-winning British female voice-over artist and she works on a vast number of projects worldwide every day. You can hear her voice on anything from video and TV narrations through to Radio and TV commercials, phone systems, automated phone answering systems, eLearning courses, aeroplanes, ships, explainer videos, cartoons, video games and much more. You may even have listened to her in some lifts scattered around the world! Della's studio is of a very high standard and uses award-winning Sontronics Aria microphone. Her voice has been described as warm and friendly with plenty of passion, meaning and panache while being crystal clear, inviting, enticing and classy. Reassuringly professional and confident, you can hear the passion in her voice in every project she undertakes. Her expertise, attention to detail and fast, quality turnaround has consistently won her new projects and repeat business, for which she is very proud.

Links:

- www.dellaphillips.com; https://twitter.com/DellaPhillips
- https://www.linkedin.com/in/della-phillips-91491315/
- https://www.instagram.com/dellaphillips/

DONNA-LOUISE BRYAN

When somebody said to me at the start that getting into the voice-over business is a marathon not a sprint, I thought that they were exaggerating. Seven years on, I can confirm that they were indeed correct.

Getting over the technical hurdles was one of the biggest challenges about entering the business for me. Not knowing what I even needed to get started, not knowing one side of a microphone from the other or WHERE to plug it in!

I felt silly asking basic questions. Like the pressure was on me to already know the answers. If I didn't, how could I even think about becoming a professional voice-over artist? Imposter syndrome was a thing for me and if I am honest, it probably held me back somewhat at the start. Although it was what I wanted, it didn't feel like a world in which I belonged.

I could have easily given up at this point and nearly did but I was driven by a desire to work alongside a genuine passion to become a professional. Before becoming an actress, I was pursuing a more academic route so I was no stranger to learning. When I did my Master's Degree in Art History, I would have to write 8,000 on subjects where I didn't even understand the title, never mind how to write 8,000 words on said title. In the end, after many strong words with myself and a heap of dogged determination, I managed to get through it. Remembering how it felt to be awarded a qualification that I had once thought was only for other people spurred me on to keep going with voice-over.

I decided to give it 6 months. Six months of reading, watching and basically learning as much as I could. If I still didn't understand after that, I would concede. Fortunately though, if you are willing to go and find it, there is a wealth of information online about all aspects of the voice-over business. By the time you are on your 50th article or YouTube video, you do slowly begin to understand what an audio interface is and why you need one. Knowledge really can be power.

I still have a great deal more to learn but it is like driving in some ways. You can still be a good driver but not fully understand the mechanics of how your car does what it does. When something does go wrong, which inevitably it will, you can search the internet, ask for help on forums or just get someone out to help you who knows more than you! Not knowing how to deal with all possible technical eventualities by yourself really should not be a barrier to getting started. I know this now!

Another hurdle was the massively conflicting advice out there for people starting out. There are strong opinions among seasoned voice-over pros on many subjects from whether those starting out in the industry should lower their prices to build their client list to what microphone is best. You respect your more experienced peers and be eager to take on board their advice but at the same time, it is easy to find yourself confused with all of the contradictions. Much of it simply comes down to personal preference.

Finding the balance between listening to the advice of my superiors and learning to take from it only what suited my individual business took courage and time.

One of my favourite jobs so far is probably an audiobook for Sage Publishing in America on the inequalities in the education system. Not only was it an honour to take on an academic subject and to help bring important issues out into the open, working with such a professional company made life so much easier. Good clients really can turn an average job into a great job. By this I mean clear consistent communication, detailed technical instructions, straightforward upload instructions etc. When starting out as a VO, you don't always have the luxury of working with the great clients out there so when they do start coming, it really does feel like you're on the right path.

I have also been working on a series of radio ads for Amazon. Again, the production house I've been working with made the sessions straightforward and fun. Clear voice direction straight into my studio via Clean Feed along with a great producer.

I have been able to use my native regional accent in these ads which I always love doing. When I became an actress, one of the first things my London agent said to me was "You can get rid of your regional accent can't you?" Over the years, I learned to neutralise my already mild Staffordshire accent and at times, hide it completely.

Any VO work that allows me to dust off my native accent is enjoyable for me and I am finding that I am getting asked more and more for Midlands or General Northern accents, especially for explainer videos and animation work.

If I could offer the 'me' that was just starting out in voice-over some advice, I would say get your head down for a long period of learning, absorb as much information as you can from various sources, both free AND paid for, and then believe in yourself enough to work out what is right for you as an individual. I would remind myself that nobody is born with the technical knowledge or the vocal skill that it takes to be a working voice talent. It has to be learned and just like I learned to drive a car or ride a horse, you CAN learn to be a voice-over artist too. There isn't a magic formula or a massive secret, it just comes down to good old-fashioned hard work.

Knowing this, that WITHIN YOU is the power, can be unbelievably liberating.

BIO:

Donna is a British voice-over artist and actress originally from Staffordshire in the Midlands and now residing in Oxfordshire with her partner, two cats, dog and horse.

Her voice is warm, clear and smooth. Great for corporate reads, IVR, medical narration, e-learning, commercial work and more, Donna can voice in Neutral RP or offer a gentle regional Midlands or General Northern lilt.

Donna has a purpose-built studio with a vocal booth. She is strong when it comes to voicing characters and she can voice everything from angry demons to kittens!

Her clients include Heathrow Airport, Boots, Sage Publishing, Siemens, Amazon, Oxford University and Tesco.

Links:

- www.voiceoverbird.co.uk
- Twitter: @donnalbryan
- Instagram: donnalouisevoiceactorpresenter

QUESTION:

What have been your main challenges?

Drop a tweet @spoonface1 and let's discuss…

ELISABETH VALENTINE

It was my childhood dream to be a voice-over artist, and I got my first voice-over job whilst I was doing my degree in music in London in 2008. I was given the opportunity to be holiday cover for the continuity speakers on one of Denmark's largest TV channels. I was both thrilled and a bit apprehensive.

My most challenging experience in the voice-over industry was largely to do with authenticity, accents and confidence. I'm from the northern part of Denmark where we have a pretty strong regional accent. Unlike the UK that embraces and celebrates its regional accents, my particular accent wasn't and probably still isn't that TV friendly.

It's a great skill to be able to speak with different accents but we sacrifice some authenticity and natural expression when adopting a different "voice". Right from the get-go, I had a sense that my natural expression wasn't "good enough" or acceptable. To be honest, I don't think my regional accent is suitable for a lot of the jobs I get. Being trained for that first TV job taught me a lot and gave me a strong foundation but also instilled in me a lot of unnatural habits and a bit of an imposter syndrome or inferiority complex. Not feeling good enough is something most of us come across in some form or another. It's certainly something I've had to work with throughout my career on different levels. First of all, I've used those feelings to fuel my desire to continuously improve. Practically that means experimenting with different techniques on my own, finding a compromise between authenticity and style, getting coaching from people who are at the top of their field, studying and not being afraid to evolve and grow.

Secondly, and this is just as important, I've said yes to jobs even when I didn't feel ready. You have to learn on the job! As much as you can prepare and practise, nothing beats actually doing it. I often can't hit the high note in a rehearsal but when I'm on stage singing, I always hit it. So I've learned to trust myself and my ability to bring the goods in the actual situation. I trust that the team around me is there to help bring out the best in me. Finally, we have to look at the factual evidence. If I wasn't good enough, I wouldn't have been offered the full-time position of being the brand voice of a national TV channel after I graduated university. If I wasn't good enough, I wouldn't have kept the job for almost 10 years now. If I wasn't good enough, I wouldn't be hired by new clients. If I wasn't good enough, clients wouldn't re-hire me. If I wasn't good enough, I wouldn't now be asked to coach other voice-over artists. And so on... We fear being perceived as arrogant but as professionals, we have to deeply know and acknowledge what we bring to the party in order for us to also charge what we're worth. If you see yourself as a professional and act accordingly, others will recognise and reward you as a professional.

My favourite projects are the ones where I get to collaborate, be creative and be challenged. The job as a voice-over artist is often a solo experience with us shut away in our little booth. So it's wonderful when I get to work in a team with a producer, a director or the client. A few jobs over the years really stand out for me... I do voices for Fisher Price toys for the Danish market, and that is always so much fun. I get to create a fun voice, use the whole scope of my vocal range and I often get to sing. I started my career as a singer and have spent years working on my craft to a very high standard, so it feels great when I can use that set of skills. And the studio and producers I get to work with on those projects are lovely.

Another job that also stood out for me was doing the localisation for a singing Just Eat commercial. The English version was already created and I did the Danish version both singing and as a VO line. It was a time-pressed and very technical job with layering vocals and harmonies that needed both precision and a near-perfect pitch. There was a huge team in the studio which was intimidating but the fact that it was challenging also made it a really satisfying job.

Finally, I did a 3 month job as a voice coach / director on a huge project for one of the world's biggest brands. I learned a huge amount by coaching the voice-over artist that I now use in my own work. I was part of a whole team and the work was incredibly detailed, precise and specific. Having high standards is something we should all strive towards.

I have a few things that I'd say to myself to do differently in the beginning but they're also applicable now. Don't be afraid to say yes. Create and update your showreels often. Enjoy it and remember that you're here to learn and grow, not to be perfect!

BIO:

Elisabeth Valentine is a voice over artist, singer, speaker and performance coach. She has been a professional performer since the age of 8 and lends her voice, expertise and coaching to some of the biggest brands in the world like Disney, Apple, Netflix, H&M, Just Eat, Virgin Atlantic, Fisher Price and My Little Pony.

Elisabeth coaches people with a focus on developing their public speaking, pitching, presentation and networking skills so then they can confidently share their message and make the biggest positive impact they can in the world.

Elisabeth is the host of the Dare, Share, Create - The Podcast with Elisabeth Valentine and the author of *Magnify Your Message, How to Become a Confident Speaker in any Situation,* coming out in 2021.

Links:

- https://instagram.com/elisabethvalentine_
- https://www.facebook.com/elisabeth.valentine
- https://www.linkedin.com/in/elisabethvalentinekristiansen/

EMMA WHEELER

When I began my Voice Over career nearly 10 years ago I had some initial coaching and recorded a demo which got me started but I felt I was thrust into the VO world with not as much knowledge as I would have liked. So for me, my most challenging experience at the beginning was dealing with the technical aspects of VO - namely the editing. These difficulties held me back for a while and I didn't feel particularly confident to forge ahead. Trying to figure out which software and how to use it was quite daunting. I knew from listening to others within the community that it was essential to have good studio equipment for providing the most efficient and quality professional Voice Over service to my potential clients.

About a year or so later a few VO companies began providing networking, workshops and webinars, conferences and on-line support to provide Voice Actors and Artists with a more in-depth learning experience covering all Voice Over areas including rates and tech knowledge and vocal care to support us whilst running our businesses.

From joining a variety of these events I found the resources and tools incredibly useful - listening to numerous informative webinars, attending workshops and conferences etc. therefore enabled me to learn so much more including on the technical side and ultimately I felt less challenged than when I had started out.

It's also advisable (especially in the early years) to seek guidance from those more experienced in the business when considering the right VO equipment. For me, it's been a work-in-progress over the years but the outcomes proved fruitful.

I think whatever level we're at in Voice Over there is always something to learn, to be informed of or perhaps refresh and explore in continuing to develop professionally which has certainly helped my business grow. So, when starting out in Voice Over seek the help and support you need to overcome those difficulties to advance forward otherwise it could hold you back. It's also good to remember there's an abundance of advice in a welcoming VO community.

I think my favourite project isn't necessarily the 'big' jobs but the ones I'm voicing which potentially help people. When I'm recording guided meditation or relaxation therapy content in my vocal booth knowing that my voice together with the script content is aiding people to feel calmer, reduce anxiety, stress and their mental health in general then this is what I find gratifying and has become a firm favourite to narrate.

I have often found when recording has finished that I myself feel calm and relaxed which is a lovely feeling to have at the end of a session I guess. Also, hopefully helping to provide listeners of the audio content with some relaxation techniques and for their lives to be a little less troubled which is an area outside of VO that I volunteer with.

As Voice Overs we talk for a living but I've also come to realise how important our 'listening' skills are.

Listening to our vocal deliveries, to direction, coaches and educators within the VO Community assists in advancing in our own business and ultimately to provide a professional service for our clients.

As mentioned earlier 2021 is my 10th year in Voice Over and being in an industry I love, involved with an amazing VO community of talented supportive people is something I'm really grateful for.

If I could return to the beginning I would have undertaken earlier in-depth coaching and delved deeper into marketing and business development which is another area I really enjoy. This would have assisted me in those earlier stages but the last 10 years have been a really great journey and looking forward to the next 10 in Voice Over.

BIO:

Emma Wheeler is a British Voice Over Artist and Singer with an English RP Voice. Having spent many years training in speech, elocution and drama through LAMDA in Birmingham she records Voice Overs from her professional home studio providing a versatile, eloquent modern voice - calm, velvety, warm, seductive, empathetic, re-assuring, smooth and inviting also when required instructional and authoritative. Her voice can assist in bringing words to life in communicating for a variety of business and creative projects.

Emma provides Voice Overs for Narration, Commercials, Corporate Video Marketing, Explainers, E-Learning Modules, Guided Meditation, Medical Narration and Public Announcements. She also voices characters for Audiobooks, Radio Drama and Animation and has written and recorded her own original song. Emma is always happy to voice the speaking elements in songs for musicians too.

To view further VO work visit www.emmawheelervoices.co.uk

Links:

- www.emmawheelervoices.co.uk/
- https://nz.linkedin.com/in/emmawheelervoiceovers
- https://www.instagram.com/voiceoveremmy/
- https://mobile.twitter.com/voiceoveremmy
- https://m.facebook.com/EmmaWheelerVoiceOvers/?locale2=en_GB
- https://www.youtube.com/channel/UCOrsKI67YXg3Er0PBgOGK-g

LORRAINE ANSELL

Being a versatile voice in a very busy market place can be daunting. There have been many challenges from technological know-how in setting up and maintaining your own studio to finding clients that you enjoy working with. As with every creative freelancer, you end up wearing many hats often at the same time. There are projects that require multiples voices, iterations of copy, time zones, teams of people for signing off and paperwork. Throw in a bit of Continuous Professional Development and you can find yourself deep into work and forget to even have lunch on some days.

The biggest challenge I have found is creating a good work/life balance. It can be thrilling and exciting to throw yourself into work and to say yes to every project that comes along. However, nowadays, I take a moment and mentally work out how much time and energy a voice project will take and plan accordingly. Long form narration, whether for e-learning projects or audio books, takes time and requires a good work flow so it is key to know up front the projects' needs and your own. Having knowledge of a project and the deliverables involved means that you can decide whether you take the job or pass on it. It has taken time and experience to gauge this and I really work hard to ensure that I work on my own personal creative projects as well as voice projects.

There have been years full of fun projects that I've worked on ranging from children's bilingual books, holiday destinations videos, apps and much more. I've learnt about random things that are helpful to me in a Zoom quiz (did you know that road sweepers come with particular watering can rose heads?). Now, back in the recesses of my mind, there are facts about the Eiffel Tower, details on software inductions, characters that live rent free coming back over and over again like a party guest who ended up staying over.

However my favourite projects are those that require fun creative input and energy from both me as the voice and from the client. When you work through a voice or the copy because something sounds a bit "almost there," together with the client you work on how to make it work and that makes for a very enjoyable time.

I recently worked on a video game character called Lady Love Dies for a game called Paradise Killer. The team asked for various voices for the copy and we re-iterated it a few times. The voice of LLD evolved into what it is now. It is my favourite because I got to play around, find the character, find her voice and thus, her words. I ended up recording the emotes as well which I love doing as it is a vocal and physical workout in the booth! The great news is that it has already been voted PC Gamer Adventure Game of the year in 2020.

In terms of writing and directing actors, I would have to say that working for Ragged Foils - a podcast for a new writing audio drama group comes to mind. I've written several pieces and had two amazing actors embody the characters. As a writer, it is always thrilling to hear your story come to life and as a director, it is satisfying talking through the copy and context with an actor and seeing how they bring their own experiences into the role. They really breathe new life into the words.

What I have learned from working with various clients and casting and directing on jobs is to work on "letting go" in many projects and to avoid overthinking. The voice-over chain is long and each point is very variable. I have auditioned a lot over the years and I have cast many voices myself. I read every brief carefully and work diligently to find the right voice(s). From advertising to explainer videos, the role of the voice is crucial but so is timing, availability etc. Sometimes it can be like playing chess in VR underwater and changing your outfits at the same time while attempting to do a quadruple tap timestep. When it comes together, the buzz is really affirming.

However, what has become so clear to me, that I would tell myself and every voice, is that every single project is uniquely subjective. So much so that most of it really exists outside of your own control. At the start, I would record a demo and agonise over the copy and then spend hours pondering and worrying about if they had heard it properly and what they thought of my voice. Having spent many years casting and directing myself now, I have realised that I should let go of that voice after sending in the demo. The reality is that there are many audio files to listen to on a given project. Having short listed so many voices, I have come to realise that the voice chosen is very subjective to me, to the production team, to the end client and to the final consumer of that voice. We all hear it differently. This means that every voice is equally valid. So I would tell the me at the start of my voice-over journey to chill out more about demos and auditions and to do the audition and be happy with that. Press send and be at peace with having done your best in the audition. The rest is as it is meant to be.

BIO:

Lorraine Ansell is an award nominated voice-over artist, director and writer. Currently featured in Lady Love Dies in Paradise Killer, Lorraine has over 20 years of experience in creative production. Known for her friendly, engaging and warm youthful voice, Lorraine works in English and Latin American Spanish. A proud Brit and Latina, Lorraine became a BAFTA member in 2020 and has been a juror for the performance categories. She has appeared in several audio dramas including Audible's Northanger Abbey. She is also a director, producer and writer of audio projects such as Ragged Foils.

Links:

- www.lorrainevoiceart.com
- Twitter: LAvoiceart
- Instagram: LivingLAvoiceart

LUCY ELLIS

I think that my most challenging experience was after I had my little boy. I put myself under a lot of pressure to get back to work. I actually did a voice session the day I came out of hospital - two days after I had had a C-section! I was really frightened that I'd lose the career I had worked so hard to build if I took too much time off so I only really gave myself a month before I started working officially again. Actually I'd still been doing bits and bobs for some of my clients all the way through anyway. I didn't realise that I needed time to find my confidence as a mum, to find myself again as a voice-over and actually to heal! I ended up on a hamster wheel of guilt, constantly trying to juggle everything and to be perfect at it all while feeling like I wasn't really doing a good job either as a mum or as a voice-over. It was a really low time.

When you work from home, there's a misconception that you can just strap your baby onto you and carry on doing your job. That may totally work for some voice-over parents but definitely not for me. I need that separation between being a mum and being Lucy. It was really hard to find a balance at first. I'm not ashamed to admit that I've had a lot of help with childcare – something I hated to start with because it made me feel like I was failure for not being able to do it all! Ridiculous! Talking really helped me get through it. Now I'm much better at talking myself out of that destructive mum guilt and having the confidence to use the flexibility that being a voice-over artist gives me in order to spend more time with my boy without feeling guilty about my work while equally allowing myself the time to focus on my work!

My favourite project is being the female voice of the Heart Network across the UK. Some people find that imaging sessions can become repetitive but I love following directions and trying to come up with new ways to deliver the messages. Most of the time it's just me connecting with my producer from my studio for sessions but we once did a live session with myself and the male imaging voice where we recorded sweepers 'as live', bouncing off each other's inflections and energy. It was such a great laugh and the audio sounded brilliant. The team I work with are really talented producers and I always get a buzz when I hear what they've created with my voice!

If I could go back to when I first started out as a voice-over artist, I think I would tell myself to be more confident and to use the opportunities I was given to promote myself more. I'm really bad at self-promotion and there have definitely been people I should have sent my demo to in the past that I didn't because I didn't think I'd done enough or was good enough. I've really learned over the years that there's no shame in letting people know you're there. I'd tell myself to stop overthinking and to send those demos!

BIO:

I've been a voice-over artist for 7 years and I'm also an experienced Radio Presenter, which is actually how I started voicing. I live by the sea on the South Coast with my husband and two year old little boy. From my lovely little garden studio I record all sorts of projects for everything from radio commercials to explainer videos, e-learning and on hold telephone messages. You can also hear me on the radio across the UK on the Heart Network as the female imaging voice for all of their Heart brands.

You can have a listen to me on my website: lucyellisvoiceover.com and you can follow me on Twitter: @LucyEllisVoice and Instagram: @lucyellisvoiceover or check out my Facebook page and You Tube Channel: Lucy Ellis Voiceover

QUESTION:

What are your main takeaways so far?

Drop a tweet @spoonface1 and let's discuss…

MALK WILLIAMS

Different people come into the world of voice-over and voice acting at different times and for different reasons. All of them face different combinations of challenges. I was changing career after spending 15 years in the IT industry and I was trying to build one up while tapering the other off.

For me, the biggest challenge was finding the right balance.

That could be deciding whether to take on an IT contract or to take a risk devoting my time to auditioning. It might be balancing how much training and equipment I could get to improve the quality of my work with how much I was actually earning from VO at the time (which wasn't much, especially considering that I had a family to support). Or it could be working out how much time to spend on each of the umpteen things that are legitimate daily work for an aspiring voice actor, whether that was auditioning, working on my website, recording new samples, sending emails to production companies or trying to work out how on Earth to make social media work for me, to name but a few. The only time I knew 100% what I had to do was when I landed a job. Then my top priority was simply to do the job to the best of my ability!

The root of the problem was that I was spreading my efforts in too many directions. In life, and in voice acting, I'm a pretty versatile person (if I say so myself!) but I needed to find a focus to build on. Deep down, I knew what that was going to be.

Ultimately, my biggest focus and my greatest strength was always audiobooks. Once I started getting noticed by a few production companies, things became a lot simpler. When each job I got took up two solid weeks, I had a lot less time to worry about what I should be doing on a daily basis, although the challenge *then* became making time to keep on marketing myself and looking to find and secure the next project while working on the current one. Voice work can be a "feast and famine" profession at the best of times, and audiobook narration is particularly prone to that.

I think that everyone starting out in voice work has similar problems with balance, especially if they have not been self-employed before. Ultimately, you need people to see you as a professional which means that you have to behave like one and organise your time. For me, that meant finding a goal to focus on, working out a path to get me there and taking steps along that path each day.

My favourite project to date… tricky. There are a lot of projects that have been my favourite at one time or another. Whether for enjoyment, for pride of achievement or just much needed funds!

However, I must put on my proverbial big boy pants and pick one. I think that it will have to be… Escape the Gloomer!

Escape the Gloomer is a narrative computer game set in the fantasy world of Redwall, based on the novels of Brian Jacques. They say that in the industry, you should never say "computer game." The term is "video game" but not in this case! It was a bit of a throwback to the world of the text-based fantasy adventure games of my youth. However, rather than typing instructions like "look around", "enter the dark cave", "open the trap door" or "pick up the iron key" and then just reading the text descriptions of the results, in Escape the Gloomer, the whole thing is narrated in audio, largely by me, along with a few character parts by other voice actors.

There were a few things that I particularly liked about it. One was that although the narration had a certain amount in common with audiobooks, the method was very different. As with most video game jobs, the lines were not in narrative sequence. As I was reading so much of it, I was able to gradually piece together the different strands of the story.

There was also a big sense of responsibility about it. Unlike an audiobook, which is pretty much down to the narrator assisted by a proofer and an editor, there was a whole development team working on this. In terms of the audio, which was the main part of the user experience, the whole thing rested more or less on my shoulders.

Finally, it was (to the best of my knowledge) the first game of its type that could be played on an Amazon Echo where it became something entirely new: an interactive audio drama, which is something I'd never heard of before. It was very exciting to be part of it. It's also the only project that I'd been in at that point to have its own trailer which is still on YouTube. You can look it up!

If I were to go back and do it all again, I think I'd do most things in a quite similar way to the first time round. I would know which courses I'd do and which I wouldn't. I'd probably get set up with a good XLR microphone right from the start, rather than get a USB microphone and then upgrade. I would get a properly designed recording booth up and running sooner than I actually did. Both of these made a huge difference to the quality of my work and my ability to work effectively. I like to think that I'd be more efficient and effective in my marketing strategy but to be honest, I still have a lot to learn on that front even now!

That's the main thing that comes to mind when I think of what I'd try to do differently. When I started out, I was pretty organized. I did my research and I made a plan. *Sticking to the plan!* That's the hard part! Not letting things slide and losing focus. So that's what I'd recommend and what I try to do as I go forward. Make a plan with verifiable short and medium term targets and stick to it. Re-evaluate it periodically to see how well you are doing, and whether some parts of your plan need to change, either because you've outgrown them or gone in a different direction. Don't just let things…

… drift.

BIO:

Malk Williams is a full time professional voice actor, voice-over and audiobook narrator based in his personal studio in the book town of Hay-on-Wye on the Welsh border. Among other credits, he has around 90 audiobooks to his name, 4 of which have been awarded Earphones Awards by AudioFile Magazine. He is a founder member of Raconteurs LLP (www.raconteurs.co.uk), a partnership of some of the UK's most accomplished audiobook narrators.

He really needs to practise what he preaches and update his website (www.malkwilliams.co.uk) and remember to occasionally post something useful on either Facebook (www.facebook.com/MalkWilliams.VoiceArtist), Twitter (www.twitter.com/MalksVoice) or
LinkedIn (www.linkedin.com/in/malk-williams).

MEL PARKER

Having worked pretty much my whole previous career in a team *and* being a sociable person by nature, the biggest challenge for me was settling in to working alone.

I chose to equip myself with a quality set up including remote recording facilities so then my voice-over work could predominantly be done from home. Although trips to recording studios *are* needed sometimes, in the main, my home set up serves me well. In turn, this can mean a lot of time spent alone!

The challenge that lone-working presents is multifaceted. On a very basic level, human interaction for me is a necessity so I work hard to make sure that I still get my fix! I attend various local networks, have my voice-over groups and friendships to meet remotely or in person when possible, while taking the opportunity throughout my working week to make sure that I'm 'seeing' people.

Problem-solving in a team environment is so much easier too, right?! You can bounce ideas off people and access the different types of thinkers present. You have the various 'experts' you might need to hand. As a lone worker, I fast learned that you have to re-create this in some form. Working alone means that *you* are every 'team' member: marketing, accounts, HR... the list goes on. So having a plan for each task and working that into my diary has really helped to manage that part of the challenge. I've found my networks (voice-over or otherwise) to be invaluable for this too. Monthly meet-ups with a small group of voice-over artists (now great friends) have helped me to tackle many a problem over the years and locally I attend a Creative Coffee networking group that has proved beneficial for my business development.

Self-motivation when working alone can be a real challenge too. It's a bonus to be able to build some of your family chores into your working day but it is very easy for the balance to tip if you're not careful. Working out what structures supported me to get on with the work in hand was a must for me. Planning my time very specifically makes sure that I don't get distracted by the non-work things....well, most of the time!

Finally, in amongst all of those layers, reminding myself that I'm never really alone helps!

There's always someone at the end of a phone or online camera and I'm never short of a willing candidate wanting to nip out for a catch up - I just have to find them!

My favourite project over the years interestingly was a rather small one but it holds a special place for me simply because of who it involved! Technology these days means that jobs with more than one voice are often done independent of each other. For the end listener, that's not always understood. So when I was asked to voice the trailer for the launch of the multi-talented Tom Hanks 'Short Stories', I was delighted!

My voice sandwiches Toms in the trailer, which always generates the question "Did you meet him to do it?" The answer is 'sadly not', but perhaps next time eh Tom?!

Often the choices we make when starting out, particularly in business, are dictated by the resources we have available. If more is available then yes, of course, I would have invested more in quality coaching (from recommended coaches in the industry) probably earlier and more frequently than I did. No doubt a wider set of voice-reels to represent the genres I wanted to focus on wouldn't have gone amiss either! Earlier investment in remote recording software much sooner than I dipped my toe would have set me on my way to those worldwide live sessions quicker than I achieved otherwise.

But the one thing that I would definitely remind myself of if I were starting over again, which interestingly costs you nothing, is to run your own race!

Yes, be aware of what others are doing and what the industry is dictating. Glance around you so then you know what everyone's up to and be in the know! But don't fall into the trap of comparing your journey to theirs or feeling that you should be taking the same or similar approach. Don't be stunted by comparison or daunted by the apparent success of others. Instead, embrace your own pace, have confidence in your own ideas and the path that you have chosen and allow your own successes to be your drive!

After all - we keep being told to stand out from the crowd, so it's cool to be a little different!

BIO:

Having enjoyed 20 years in Public Sector Management, I thought that I would escape my corporate roots. However, I fast realised that embracing them was the key to my success in the voice-over industry.

All those years ago - transferring my previous skills and marrying them with newly developed ones - paved the way to me now loving voicing and supporting projects predominantly in the Corporate Sector for numerous clients worldwide, peppered with some commercial work too for good measure!

Lots more information about my work and an opportunity to listen in can be found on my website https://melsbritishvoice.co.uk/

Please do catch up with me on:

- Twitter: @MelsBritishVOs
- Insta: @MelsBritishVoice
- LinkedIn: Mel Parker (or Mel's British Voice)

NANO NAGLE

After working in the theatre all my life, I could see that as I grew older, I would need to find another outlet for my creativity as there wasn't a lot of work for the older woman! A lovely director friend of mine said, "Get into audiodrama! You'll love it......" So the more I thought about it, the more I said to myself, "Why not?" This could fulfil a creative need and I loved change. I cannily thought that starting in audiobooks would be something that I would have more control over and so my journey began. What type of challenge I had set myself, I really had no idea; it was immense. The only voice-overs I had done in the past were in a studio and totally controlled by a sound engineer. Now I was going to have to set up a sort of studio and learn about SOUND and how to capture it as well as perform. In my naivety, I was not phased as the internet was full of advice and I was secure in my ability to act, so I jumped in. Firstly I found ACX, which was a place to put yourself out there and to advertise your wares so to speak, if you wanted to narrate self-published eBooks. I had the idea that this is where I could practise. I was confident, let me tell you. I laugh thinking back as I just had no idea about the industry at all.

I bought a USB microphone and set it up to my iPad where I found an app which helped me record. My sound-proofing was practically non-existent and my ears were just not attuned to the peripheral sounds that I was picking up because I was acting my little socks off as if I was on stage and not in the intimacy of a spoken word book! To my astonishment, American authors on ACX asked me to narrate. At first, it was exciting and I said yes, yes and yes. This was until I realised that some of the authors used grammar and text that was just not literary and impossible to bring to life. I had to turn the books down and realised that my very talented technological savvy son would have to help me. Of course, he then had to teach himself from the internet about voice-overs and setting up a home studio.

I had to explain to my son that we had to go through this slowly and that I needed to have my hand held. I wrote everything down and sound-proofed a small space. I practised and practised and learnt about editing and recording. I can hardly believe that I had books published through ACX but I did and I am forever grateful to the authors and sound engineers because I learnt what I didn't know. That allowed me to find the right microphone, preamp and DAW. I felt proud of myself, really proud, but there was something missing and that was my ability to tone down my acting to better interpret the narrative and characters of the novels that I was producing. This was the biggest challenge for me and the way that I remedied this was by finding a coach/mentor who was a voice-over actor. Slowly I began to hear where I was out of synch with this medium and how I needed to be a director and overseer of my work.

This was just the beginning of course but I had passed the challenge and was being asked to voice/narrate more and more, and actually had positive reviews on Audible. This brings me to my favourite project that carries this journey of mine forward to this day.

My first paid per finished hour audiobook, rather than a royalty share, came from a lovely author who had a series of books set in the Viking and Saxon period. I jumped with joy when reading them. They were well-written and the history really interested me. I was well thought of and she was full of praise. Still to this day, Octavia Randolph uses me to narrate and with every book she writes, I find more subtleties and grow the characters as they age and tread their path in life. This particular series has helped me with every piece of audio that I have recorded since, whether it be games, audioguides, animations or e-learning.

As I look back on the way I entered the voice-over industry, I smile and see how difficult and anxious I was and how it was completely unnecessary. Why didn't I just find a coach who could see me through each and every stage? Because I had worked in the theatre for so long, I did not understand how very different this acting was and I was arrogant about changing my perceptions. I needed to have a more accepting humble approach. There are so many knowledgeable professionals out there that can help so I should have taken my time and found that wizard first. They would have understood and it wouldn't have taken me so long. On the other hand, I learnt to listen to my work dispassionately and my self-directing skills have enhanced my work.

BIO:

Links:
Website:
www.nanovoiceartist.co.uk

Spotlight:
https://www.spotlight.com/interactive/cv/9653-7863-5769

NOELLE ADAMES

"If you ask me what I came into this life to do, I will tell you:
I came to live out loud."

- Emile Zola

What has been my most challenging experience?

Trusting myself. I am a physical actor and do a lot of character work on stage. I enjoy experimenting with voices and where I put the energy of my character in my body changes how a character talks and sounds. When I was new to voice-over, I wanted to play it safe and I wasn't sure what was expected of me. I would do a first read without any characterisation at all, which was very flat. I was waiting for the director to tell me what to do. This worked fine with directors who wanted to work with my voice as it was, mostly commercials, but I booked a commercial and after the first read, I could tell that the director was disappointed that I had not made any choices of my own. They never hired me again. I have become more comfortable looking at a piece of work as more of a collaboration between me, the director, the technician and client. I now communicate what I am doing so then I can be 'on the same page' as the director – 'I am going to do a plain read so you can hear what my voice sounds like and we can go from there" or "I've really been playing with this and have a few ideas, here's one. They will tell you what they are looking for, so it's alright to communicate your ideas. In acting, I know to make really bold choices about the characters and I now trust myself to do this with voice work as well.

I did the same with auditions in the beginning. I would submit a plain read. Now I know to submit two audition pieces; one a straight forward read and one where I really make strong, bold choices. I get to really have fun and it shows. I love it when I am asked to do audition recordings for all of the voices in the piece. I get to really choose different voices for each character. I learned how to prep for multiple characters when I was researching audio books – highlighting each character in a different colour and knowing what their personality and accent is. In terms of moving and finding that character in my body, I definitely do this with voice work but I am aware that too much movement may be heard in the recording. I focus the energy of the character into smaller movements or where in my mouth the sound is coming from, and also if my body is stiff or loose, full or thin etc. Try it, right now. How does your voice sound if your body is very full and the sound comes from the back of your throat? What about a very thin, empty body with the sound coming from the front of your mouth?

I was involved in a project with other voice artists from Spoons Voices called "Love Jumps." The concept and main characters were agreed upon by the creators, and we were hired to bring the story and new characters to life. What was amazing about this project was that before we began, we were asked to share any thoughts or ideas about the situations and characters that would move the plot along. When we arrived to record, we had a quick discussion about what the next scene was going to be about and just jumped into improvising. I already felt connected to the project because I had provided my ideas and the rest felt like play. I learned a lot about listening to other characters (giving them the focus), playing with my voice, judging my own timing of when to enter or leave a scene and how to work together. Listening to the other actors take risks, sound silly, make mistakes and try new things gave me the "permission" to do so. It was a creative, fun experience where we also made a super cool series about relationships.

What would I tell myself to do differently if I could go back?

Don't wait. Before I moved to London, I was acting in Los Angeles and had lots of friends who were in the voice acting industry. Back then, it felt like some mysterious nether world that was out of my grasp. I don't even know why I thought that. After I had been living in London for a few years, I saw a workshop being offered on voice-over and I thought I would take the first step. It was really helpful in that we each took turns doing a voice recording and received feedback. We learned about how the industry works but the most important thing I heard that day was "Just do it", "Play", "Learn about **your** voice", "Be yourself"... All things that I knew but needed to hear from a professional. The workshop solidified ideas that had been floating around in my mind and made them real, which was the experience I needed to move forward with my career. The unknown became known. What do you need to take your first or next step? I was aware that a good voice reel is the key to having my voice listened to when clients are searching for artists. After the workshop, I made sure that I went to a professional experienced technician to have a commercial reel made. Next, I read everything that I could about voice work, watched videos, listened to speakers, learned about the equipment and joined voice-over groups. I was constantly learning from others. Despite all this, I was still very nervous during the first few jobs but for me, knowledge is power. The more I knew, the better I felt. I am still constantly learning and I would say that the one thing that has changed is that I ask more questions, want clarification and then play!

BIO:

Noelle Adames is an LA transplant. London has been a very exciting place for Noelle to work. You can hear her voice on projects such as Alfa Romeo, Neuvana, Nescafe and Love Jumps. She recently completed work on an ITV Marilyn Monroe biopic and played Titania in the cutting-edge live stream of 'A Midsummer Night's Dream' with 60 Hour Shakespeare. Other London performances include a fun show with Slackline Productions at the Southwark Playhouse and the Eagle and Beaver Ensemble at the Union Theatre. She had wonderful experiences performing in the US with the Will Geer Theatricum Botanicum in Topanga, CA. As well as theatre, her film and television credits include ITV – Biopic: Marilyn Monroe, Eleventh Hour (Warner Brothers), Firelight and Scenes from Oblivion.

Links:

- Spotlight: https://www.spotlight.com/profile/5818-6756-4216
- Twitter: @NoelleAdamesLon
- Insta: noelleadames_londonactress

PAUL J ROSE

When Spoon first approached me to contribute to this book, I thought that he'd made a mistake. His message said that he was writing a book featuring leading VO talent. Leading? Hardly. For one thing, 'leading' is just one of those marketing phrases that really doesn't mean anything at all. This isn't a race so how exactly does one lead?

Nonetheless, I am both flattered and honoured to be a part of it. I've been a voice-over artist for a little over 30 years now, although it's worth mentioning that 24 of those years have also included my 'proper job'. The vast majority of voice-over projects were done in the evenings or on weekends. I made a point of never taking more than one week's full holiday so then if I needed the occasional half day here and there to go into a studio, it was never a problem.

Spoon asked me to think about the most challenging experience I›ve had in the voice industry. Truth be told, over the span of 30 years, the challenges have changed. When I started out, my biggest challenge was that I didn't get it.

I had always played around with silly voices. From my earliest school days, I took part in shows which called upon me to alter my voice and create new characters. It was just fun for me and it wasn't until the late 1990s when my friends and relatives started to suggest that I should find a way to make money from this skill.

I read some books about voice-over and got in touch with some artists whose careers I aspired to. To any of them reading this book, I would like to say thank you. You were generous with your time and advice and I like to think that you inspired me to react in the same way when people now come to me, seeking advice on how to become a full time voice-over.

So what was it that I just didn't 'get'? Well, I approached this industry with a very blinkered view. As someone who had played around with characters and impersonations, I called animation studios, video game production companies and advertising agencies. I had a simple ambition – to be the voice of a famous cartoon character. Quickly that was adapted to being the voice of a cartoon character and ultimately to 'just getting hired please'. I built a website, created my own demos and just kept knocking on doors.

And got nowhere.

I had missed one crucial step in the ladder to becoming a voice-over. In fact, you could argue that I had missed several. Listing my mistakes in no particular order; I produced my own demo by throwing a multitude of impressions together, I had not looked into getting any coaching and I had not made any attempt to market the one voice which would go on to be the foundation of my career – my own, natural speaking voice.

I found a voice-over masterclass, being run by Gary Terzza, who at the time was working as a continuity announcer at Channel 4. His masterclass involved working together in a studio to put together a series of demos and in doing so, to discover the niche markets to which my voice was best suited.

As we worked together, Gary asked me if I had ever looked at doing corporate work. Such opportunities rarely excited me. I was a member of a Pay to Play website called Voice123 but I tended to skip those auditions because I didn't really feel that I was best suited to them.

Gary told me I was wrong. Twenty-five years in sales and sales training had given me a natural 'corporate voice', so I started auditioning for more of those jobs. It turned out that this was what I should have been doing all along.

But something interesting happened too. I was working with more production companies who, once happy with my work, checked out what else I could do. It wasn't long before those same companies were asking me to create characters and do impersonations. It was an organic process but over time I recognised that while I still had that dream of being the voice of a famous cartoon character, it was no longer the driving force behind my work. I was paying my bills through voice-over work and I reinvested in more coaching – this time with the brilliant Nancy Wolfson of Braintracks Audio – a lady I will never be able to thank enough. In 2014, I was able to step away from the 'proper job' and take the plunge into doing this full time.

My favourite project

We all get asked this question and I often struggle to find the answer because there are so many wonderful projects with which I have been involved. However, there is one that is very special to me.

I've been the voice of Santa Claus across numerous projects. From telephone systems to in store announcements, TV and radio commercials and charity appeals – you name it.

A few years ago, I offered to call a good friend's children on Christmas Eve and to talk to them as Santa. After just one phone call, I came out of my studio, turned to my wife and said, "I could do this all day." There's just something truly magical about becoming Santa Claus. I had tried putting on the suit and working in a real life grotto and I have to tell you that the whole experience is far less than pleasant. A conveyer belt of families who each get about 2 minutes being asked the same questions before being whisked away to buy a bunch of plastic tat that they really don't want.

I wanted to give the children a better experience. Santa shouldn't have to ask them if they've been naughty or nice. He's supposed to know – after all, he has the list and he's checked it. Twice. That's why I interview the parents ahead of the call and learn everything about their children. The effect is truly magical. They simply cannot conceive of the notion that their parents had hired an actor. If he says he's Santa, talks like Santa and knows the stuff that only Santa could know, he must be Santa.

I now run this project as a business and 2020 was my busiest year yet. No surprise really, as there were no grottos this year, so Santacallz provided many families with a wonderful alternative.

Today

If I could go back and tell my younger self to do things differently, I'd tell him to invest in coaching and in a professionally produced demo reel. Moreover, I would tell him that there is a danger when working in the creative profession of getting into a very poor business cycle.

You market yourself, then you get a job and you celebrate that win. While you're celebrating, you're not marketing. It is a pattern seen all too often and it's an important habit to break.

Voice-over is a business – if I was looking to hire someone to do my sales for me, would I be happy with my own sales performance as a measure? The hard truth is that I wouldn't be. Being self-employed means that you must wear many hats. The two most important ones are marketing and production. If you fail to produce good quality work on time, people will not hire you again and if you fail to market yourself effectively, people will not hire you in the first place.

BIO:

You can check out my website at www.pauljrose.co.uk

I'm on Facebook at www.facebook.com/pauljrosevoices and www.facebok.com/pauljrosevoiceover

I'm on LinkedIn at www.linkedin.com/in/pauljrosevoiceover

Whilst we could continue with the likes of Twitter, Instagram and whatever else gets invented by the time this goes to print, those are the ones I am most active on.

I'd like to thank Spoon once again for letting me be a part of this project and I hope that you're enjoying reading it so far.

RAMESH MAHTANI

I am an optimist and always have been. I've tried not to let anything prevent me from reaching my goals. However, I can point out a couple of hurdles, or perhaps better phrased, challenges that have come my way. The first is so deeply embedded in Western psyche that it may take a long time for it to be washed out, if at all. The second is partly related to the first, and it is one that I have successfully overcome and turned to my advantage.

The first challenge points to the cultural bias that is so deeply rooted within Western society. In an anonymous world where a voice hirer often only sees a name tagged to an audition, they may wonder if you really are the real McCoy. When your name doesn't sound like your average white name, people question if you really are a "native" speaker. I think I have lost the ball many times in this scenario where I would have possibly been hired if my name was a little more "white-sounding." Early on in my career, my family and I discussed adopting a stage name for that particular reason. After much debate, I decided to stick to my real name.

The second hurdle turned out well for me. When I started out in voice-over, I was desperate to try and fit into a mould; to tick the right box, that sort of thing. There were only so many boxes you could tick. Mine didn't really exist back then. I am a natural English speaker with English being my first language. I am a multi-cultural, ethnically diverse person with an accent that I wasn't quite sure where to place, However, I was constantly trying to pigeon-hole my accent as *British UK*, which is the closest to what I thought it sounded like. But it didn't *sound* 100% British, which clients and agents alike could tell; it wasn't American or Indian altogether. I got frustrated attempting to fit a round peg into a square hole. It gradually dawned on me that I should start to embrace my uniqueness. To use it in my favour, rather than swimming cross-current to a shore that probably would never welcome me. The world has become a little more inclusive and I have slowly overcome my feelings of awkwardness regarding my accent. I have wholeheartedly embraced the attributes of my "International English" voice with its uniqueness and global appeal.

With time and a penchant to constantly improve and sharpen my skills, it's been wonderful to see how I've been able to adapt and change my accent *at will.* My core accent remains to be what we have now established as "Neutral English" or "International English", which is different to the Mid-Atlantic American-British hybrids of the Cary Grants and Katharine Hepburns. I can now realistically "put on" a general American or UK English accent while feeling totally confident that it does sound like the real McCoy.

At the end of the day, it all boils down to putting forward your best professional self. This also means wanting to learn, improve and ensure that what the client hears leaves them downright impressed, with absolutely no doubt that your recordings are free of mispronunciations, slip ups and audio glitches.

Today I run a successful business as a voice-over, project manager, studio engineer (of sorts) and casting director. My client list includes some from my very early days and others that have become faithful repeat clients over the years, confident that they can trust my ear and judgement in getting the exact voice for their projects.

I must say that what I love most is doing accent work. I have had to be able to do various Indian English roles for the same project, putting on various flavours and intensities of Indian accent. At the same time, I have had to put on Spanish and French accents. These types of jobs are hugely fun and rewarding for me because I have to act, bring out the talent from within and sound 100% believable.

What would I do differently?

I would have taken greater pains in the technical aspects of the soundproofing of my booth. Although my present studio sounds wonderful, I'm still a little wary of low flying helicopters or a neighbour's leaf blower during a client-directed session. It's never too late to improve!

BIO:

The son of Indian parents, Ramesh grew up in the Canary Islands, Spain, the UK and the USA. His career as a voice-over artist spans over 20 years, a large component of which is public speaking. His work experience ranges from investment banking at Goldman Sachs through to NGO's. Thanks to his multi-cultural diversity, Ramesh is able to create the right persona to sound convincing and real, in English, Spanish or French. He works from professional home studios in either Spain or the UK with state-of-the-art equipment. His warm and friendly personality combined with efficiency and attention to detail have helped him consolidate his global VO career in Europe and beyond.

Links:

- www.rameshmahtani.com
- https://vimeo.com/user26297426
- https://twitter.com/Rameshmahtanivo
- https://www.linkedin.com/in/omnieuro

- https://www.facebook.com/omnieuro/
- https://www.youtube.com/channel/UCN41MDjKV3YOHMMzvtGj9Qw
- https://www.instagram.com/rameshmahtanivo/

QUESTION:

What do you feel your next steps could be?

Drop a tweet @spoonface1 and let's discuss…

THOMAS MACHIN

First starting out, taking that first step (not just as a voice actor), is the most difficult and challenging part of beginning your working life. The self-doubt and not being sure how to do anything can be crippling. Even after training, being sure that you are good at what you do and having practical experience still means that self-doubt tries to disguise itself as 'being humble'. This is a mountain that can move in front of you at the last minute. Our biggest and most important job as voice actors, is auditioning for roles. We need to figure out what everyone else is doing and give them something fresh and unique while staying true to the concept of the client. The average number of times that you audition increases each time. The more you audition, the better your chances of winning that role. Here's the rub. Rejection should be like water off a duck's back. Does a waitress feel bad because you didn't order the pie? While you never get a second chance to make a first impression, most clients won't remember your name or who you are. It's not personal. In fact, it's about as impersonal as you can get these days. Starting out is a huge freedom and one that is more forgiving of you than you are.

The best advice I got when I was first getting started was "Ready, Shoot, Aim." There is a whole philosophy behind the statement that would take well over 1000 words to explain alone. The basic concept is to just do it and then to make adjustments. Then, do it again until you start hitting the bull's eye consistently. Once you find out what works, keep doing it. "Stop doing the things that don't work and find things that do. Do more of those things that work, and less of what doesn't."

Out of all the projects I've done to date, writing and producing full-cast audios has been an absolute joy. The casting of the talent is actually tougher than expected but the talent always seems to amaze me to this day. Putting it all together with the sound design for the final production... There is no finer feeling than to be able to step through each stage knowing that without the talent of those involved, I couldn't have done it by myself. Even though I've done voice acting for animation, commercials, video games, full-cast audio productions and audiobooks, I find producing to be the most satisfying. Take careful notice that at no point did I say that any of it was easy or a 'snap' to accomplish. Each thing takes a ton of time and effort. Frustration and self-doubt can be your enemies. Just keep your eyes on the goal/s and you will win.

Second guessing yourself is one thing, but often we are asked about IF we did things differently, what we would do. You know, "If you could travel back in time and talk with your younger self…" Getting away from the fortune cookie answers is not as easy as you'd think. But here's the short of it. I came from an era that required you to not skimp on training or your gear/environment. Luckily, the same goes today. My problem was I went straight for the "Throw money at it" type of solution instead of breaking back into things slowly. I did think about that but then realized quickly that if I put in a huge investment into doing the work, my work would suffer from commitment-itus. I not only had to have the mental and emotional desire but the bamboo shoots under my fingernails also had to keep me motivated.

I've gone from voice work to video production to computers/networks and working in each area for substantial periods of time. I've had a few businesses ranging from computer animation in the early days when an expensive silicon graphics computer was required, to hardening the networks of international banks. It was in my last endeavor of computers/ networks that I made enough money that it allowed me to semi-retire. It was from there, that I used the cash to get my booth, gear and most importantly, training. Of course, some went towards having demos done when I was told it was time. The bottom line is important from start to finish. While I've made the investment back (and then some), there was a time I wondered if it would pan out.

So, my advice would be to have patience, to be diligent and to have faith that things will work out… oh, and that ACX/Audible thing will blow over just like 2020 did.

BIO:

Thomas Machin, a full time professional voice actor and producer, lives near Indianapolis. After receiving his Bachelors in Radio/TV and Advertising (Marketing) and a Masters in Electrical Engineering Technologies with several security certifications and clearances, he worked as one the first computer video editors and animators in the state. He found that computers were running everything and formed a business for computer network security. After several decades, he sold off his computer network security business and used the funds to go back to his first love: voice acting and production. Thomas began doing audiobooks, multiple character voices for animation and video games, and endless TV/Radio commercials (and PSA's). In 2017, he started MagePro Studios with his wife, where he does audio clean-up for all sorts of productions, full cast audios and helps other voice actors on top of his regular voice acting.

He can be contacted through:
https://magepro.com/talent/talent-thomas-machin/.

You can also find Thomas at…

LinkedIn: https://www.linkedin.com/in/thomasmachinvo/
AND
https://www.linkedin.com/company/magepro-studios

Facebook: https://www.facebook.com/thomas.machin.106
AND
https://www.facebook.com/MageProStudios

He is represented by Impressive Voices / Impressive Talent (https://www.impressivetalent.com/voice_over_artist/talent/642/thomas)

info@impressivevoices.com or 310-922-2900 and ask for Lisa (Thomas 3 or Thomas M)

He has been described as….
Funny, engaging and relaxing like a Hannah Barbara cartoon actor.
Authoritative
Biscuits… mmmmm, biscuits
Multifaceted
Wise
Authentic

VICKY TESSIO

I suppose that all of us - voice talents and artists in general - could write a list of challenging experiences in our careers...

To me, the most challenging moment happened when I decided to train in voice acting here in the UK, even while knowing that my English skills were far from polished.

I started my career as a VO artist in Spain in 2004 so when I moved to London 6 years ago, I already had experience in the business. But I knew that I wanted to keep learning and I wanted to take advantage of the amazing possibilities that this city has to offer. So despite all of my fears and insecurities, despite the fact that my English was not at a high level, I decided to jump into this completely uncomfortable zone and keep growing as a professional and as a person.

To train in a craft in which words are an essential ingredient, and doing it in a different language than your native one is an enormous challenge itself. Add to that the complexities of acting, and that demands high levels of vulnerability and exposure.

I can't deny that it was not an easy academic year for me: picture yourself in the middle of a storm, trying to deal with the wind and the rain while you're on a muddy ground. Pretty much like that. Sometimes you fall and you're not able to move, and most of the time you can only keep going on all fours. Even when you are able to stand up and advance, you're still feeling that you're failing miserably.

Being an introverted person in a foreign country, I was conscious that I was about to start a high risky path. But I went for it. I trained in different genres and techniques: Vocal Intensive and Vocal Extreme with Yvonne Morley. Character Voices for Animation with Dian Perry, ADR at Warner Bros De Lane Lea Studios, Impromptu Character Development with Stephane Cornicard and of course, Character Development for Video-games with Dave Fennoy.

As a result of that process (2016/2017), I won a Voice Arts Award for

Outstanding Animation/Gaming Demo Reel, Best Spanish Performance. That was in November 2017.

I also ended up completely burned-out two years later.

Here are my reflections on all of that.

- A potential is not a fact.

The seeds of what you are capable of are already inside of you. A seed needs good soil to start growing, so be aware of your mindset before starting any sowing plans.

Adding some food, and light, and water will make your seed start growing some roots. Nothing will be visible yet but the roots are essential. You need always roots before you can grow a plant. But remember, having a plant today doesn't mean that you can stop caring. You need some time and care to get fruit.

Having a plant today doesn't mean that you can stop caring. Respect and honour the process.

- There's no such thing as a "compartmentalised" life: everything you do can help you in your journey.

Years ago, I started to realise that everything I'd learnt over the years, related or not with my professional path, is interconnected. Studying music as a child helped me to understand rhythm and melody structures, and you can see that on a script. Tai Chi taught me the importance of failure and repetition when training, in addition to going the extra mile to obtain better results. Swimming has improved my breathing capacity... Going through some difficult experiences in life has taught me some important things about myself and about others, and you can apply that at work and in life.

Training in a foreign language - which meant putting myself in a very vulnerable position - felt like stretching my brain to unexpected limits. As a result, my acting skills improved dramatically in my own language, Spanish. It also became easier for me to be calm and focused in an audition or a directed session.

Confidence is a muscle. It can be trained and reinforced. That's why my advice would be to choose the things that scare you, prepare to feel absolutely uncomfortable, and go through them. You will grow exponentially.

- For the same reason, everything you do can damage your process.

Nobody can do everything alone. We know we are wired for connection, not only in our personal life but also in our professional one. Please, let's stop accepting ideas like "If you don't succeed, it is your fault", "Everything depends on you" etc. In my opinion, those mottos perpetuate a toxic work culture that includes burnout, depression and abuse.

We live in a community. We are a community. That means we have duties and rights. One of our duties is to support each other, and one of the more critical ways to do that is staying strong together against whoever tries to undermine our profession. Starting with rates: never undersell your work.

What about rights? "I can't believe I still have to protest this shit." To have some time to relax, to sleep well, to eat well, to go for a walk, to have a hobby and to spend time with the people we love. To ask for help and support, and to get it.

Let's stop our 24/7 availability. Respect and honour yourself.

In 2019, I co-founded a company called VivaVoice.UK, along with Spanish sound designer Chusé Fernandez. We have made some nice projects like "Para Que Tú Me Oigas" (So You Can Hear Me) based on a poem by Pablo Neruda with which we won a Voice Arts Award 2020 for Outstanding Spoken Word or Storytelling, Best Spanish Performance.

My favourite project is our recreation of the classic "El Principito" (The Little Prince), an audiobook we've produced using different voices, immersive sound design and music specifically created for this production. I am extremely happy and proud of this work, and it was a joy for me to play the narrator as well as the Little Prince himself.

https://www.vivavoice.uk/el-principito-audiolibro

What would I do differently if I could?

I would choose 3 words that I heard from my dear colleague Elroy 'Spoonface' Powell that deeply resonated with me: #GiveYourselfPermission.

BIO:

Vicky Tessio is a multi-award winning EU Spanish Voice Actor and Director based in London.

She started to work as a voice-over artist in 2004 after a long career in Media, especially Radio.

She is also the Co-Founder and Director ofVivaVoice UK, a sound production company focused on the Spanish Culture.

Links:

- www.vickytessio.com
- www.vivavoice.uk
- Facebook: https://www.facebook.com/vicky.tessio/
- Twitter : https://twitter.com/SpainSpanishVO
- Instagram : https://www.instagram.com/vickytessiospanishvo/
- Linkedin: https://www.linkedin.com/in/vickytessio/
- Youtube: https://www.youtube.com/user/VickyTessioLocutora

ELROY 'SPOONFACE' POWELL - SPOON THE VOICE GUY

"Without a sense of purpose, balance and inner peace, what does it all really mean?"

- Spoon The Voice Guy

I started my voice career as a number one selling artist. In 2000, there was a Barry White sample on a house groove tearing up the Balearics. My vocal coach at the time, Lisa Millet, was signed to massive dance label Defected. She was well connected in that world and knew the producers. The guys that put the song together wanted a commercial release but the legendary voice of love didn't want to give permission for his vocals to be used and that's where I came in. To borrow a phrase, 'My world got flipped-turned-upside-down'.

I ended up heading out to Italy with Lisa coaching me through the hardest vocal session of my life. Fast-forward and it became a smash hit worldwide, topping the charts in the UK.

I had never experienced this level of success or access to the music industry before.

I learned loads from travelling, performing and soaking up the business but I was also burned out from trying to balance work, my family and making a living.

There was a heavy weight to bear at times in terms of the expectations around the music that I should be making. It was only when I let go of chasing chart success and pleasing others that things changed. I touch on this in my book 'How To Think Beyond A Chart Position' (https://bit.ly/5keyspoon)

Starting from ground zero years later, I began to focus on acting and voice-overs.

The toughest decision I made was transitioning from singing to voice-acting as a primary focus. But why? Can't you just do it all? Of course you can and I still do but in order to maintain balance, I had to separate singing/song-writing for a living and the joy I get from it as a creative, cathartic vehicle of expression.

The voice acting industry is very different to being a musician. There's a culture of 'on-spec-work-for-free' that makes it incredibly hard to earn a living. The Musicians Union regularly hears from artists being asked to work for free, as much as 71% at the time of writing this.

When I realised I had to make that choice and could give my self permission to make that move guilt free, it all fell into place and the stress dissolved away.

There are so many fun and exciting projects I've been involved with from video games to commercials but one of my favourites is Current Account Switch Guarantee (CASS).

It started around 2016 and I love this project because I get to sing and use the natural parts of my speaking voice. The team are also great to work with and I always look forward to sessions with them.

My very first voice-over sessions were in the late 1990's for Trouble Television, a teen channel owned by Virgin Media at one point. I did a ton of channel idents and stings as a voice both behind and in front of the camera. I then got my break in the music industry and focused more on song writing and performance. The Halifax Howard and Egg Internet banking campaigns happened after the number one record but I got so absorbed in the music making world that I didn't follow up as much as I could have. It didn't feel like there were enough hours in a day. I'd definitely go back and tell myself to keep doing loads of voice-over / voice acting sessions with consistency.

There are some other key elements I'd put in place for sure.

Build a team and do more community focused-work, but the most important would be to pause. Take mindful moments and more time to reflect.

We can often be surrounded by a lot of 'noise' externally and internally.

Making a conscious effort to slow down and take time to ourselves can do so much to provide clarity and offer healing.

The ability to let go of stress and to re-wire the responses that we have to our fears can make a world of difference to the quality of our life and experiences.

In my opinion, this is at the heart of creating a sustainable career.

References:

- https://www.theguardian.com/music/2020/may/09/we-shouldnt-just-be-used-for-charity-musicians-are-still-getting-work-but-theyre-not-being-paid
- https://www.musicmindsmatter.org.uk/the-study/
- https://musiciansunion.org.uk/campaigns/fighting-for-fair-pay-for-musicians
- https://www.voices.com/company/press/reports

BIO:

Elroy 'Spoonface' Powell (Spoon), the voice behind club anthem 'Hey Girl', had his first taste of international recording success as part of the EDM group 'Black Legend'. Their reworking of the Barry White classic 'You See the Trouble with Me' reached No. 1 in the UK and sold over a million copies worldwide. Spoon is now an actor and leading voice-over artist. He has appeared in the hit Christmas movie, 'Jingle Jangle', Stephen Merchant and Dwayne 'The Rock' Johnson's Film 'Fighting With My Family', 'Star Wars: The Force Awakens' plus a number of campaigns for high-end brands.

Outside of his acting and voice career, Spoon is a fan of martial arts, wellness and community projects. His book 'How To Think Beyond A Chart Position' is currently available on Amazon.

Links:

- spoonsvoices.com
- instagram.com/spoonface1
- twitter.com/spoonface1
- linkedin.com/in/spoonface1
- https://bit.ly/5keyspoon
- https://r4dstore.com

WOULD YOU LIKE TO CONTRIBUTE?

Voice Over Secrets 2 is open to featuring more VO artists.

Please email *info@thesuccesstips.com* and we will send you our Contributor Guide. Basically it would be an article of 1000 words, a short author bio and a high resolution headshot.

Voice Over Secrets is available on Kindle, Audible and paperback via Amazon.

Published by FAADA

Photo: Spoon The Voice Guy at work, Hard Rock Hotel Maldives, January 2021

Printed in Great Britain
by Amazon

22613932R00055